What Floats?

words by Jill McDougall
photographs by Martin Smith

What will float?

Will this float?

Yes. It floats.

Will this float?

No. It sinks.

Will this float?

Yes. It floats.

Will this float?

Yes. It floats.

Will this float?

No. It sinks.

Will this float?

Yes it floats.

But it gets wet.

Then it sinks.